James Webb Space Telescope

A Peek into the First Galaxies

Diane Lindsey Reeves

Lerner Publications ◆ Minneapolis

Lerner Publications Company
An imprint of Lerner Publishing Group, Inc.
241 First Avenue North
Minneapolis, MN 55401 USA

For reading levels and more information, look up this title at www.lernerbooks.com.

Main body text set in Aptifer Sans LT Pro.
Typeface provided by Linotype.

Library of Congress Cataloging-in-Publication Data

Names: Reeves, Diane Lindsey, 1959– author.
Title: James Webb Space Telescope : a peek into the first galaxies / Diane Lindsey Reeves.
Description: Minneapolis, MN : Lerner Publications, [2024] | Series: Alternator books. Space explorer guidebooks | Includes bibliographical references and index. | Audience: Ages 8–12 | Audience: Grades 4–6 | Summary: "The James Webb Space Telescope orbits the sun, is one hundred times more powerful than the Hubble, and lets scientists see back in time. Learn all about the JWST in this thrilling book"— Provided by publisher.
Identifiers: LCCN 2023005590 (print) | LCCN 2023005591 (ebook) | ISBN 9798765609064 (library binding) | ISBN 9798765617823 (epub)
Subjects: LCSH: James Webb Space Telescope (Spacecraft)—Juvenile literature. | Space telescopes—Juvenile literature. | BISAC: JUVENILE NONFICTION / Science & Nature / Astronomy
Classification: LCC QB500.269 .R449 2024 (print) | LCC QB500.269 (ebook) | DDC 522/.2919—dc23/eng20230714

LC record available at https://lccn.loc.gov/2023005590
LC ebook record available at https://lccn.loc.gov/2023005591

Manufactured in the United States of America
1 – CG – 12/15/23

TABLE OF CONTENTS

THE WONDER OF IT ALL

Have you ever gone outside on a clear, dark night to look at the sky? You see the moon and bright groups of stars called constellations. With a little luck and the right timing, you might

The night sky is full of wonders to discover.

spot other planets, comets, asteroids, and meteors. Look long enough and you can't help but wonder:

What else is up there?

That's exactly what the James Webb Space Telescope (JWST) is meant to find out. This technological marvel takes scientists beyond what we see in the night sky to provide glimpses of the far-away universe. For the first time ever, we can see images from more than 13 billion light years away!

Scientists are eager to learn all they can about galaxies beyond. What will they discover next?

The Hubble Space Telescope orbits around Earth every 95 minutes.

CHAPTER 1

IT STARTED WITH HUBBLE

Like all brilliant innovations, the Hubble Space Telescope started with an idea: What could we discover if we launched a large telescope into space? This idea was first mentioned in 1946 by an astrophysicist named Lyman Spitzer Jr.

His idea got lost in the shuffle as satellites and space probes took center stage. The Soviet Union was first to launch satellites with Saturn 1 and 2 in 1957. Sputnik 2 carried the first living creature into space. It was a dog named Laika!

Stamp celebrating Laika, the Soviet spacedog that traveled on Sputnik 2.

FIRST SATELLITE

The National Aeronautics and Space Administration (NASA) launched the first US satellite in 1958. It was called Explorer 1. It orbited Earth 58,000 times before it was destroyed when it reentered the earth's atmosphere in 1970. Over the years, even more powerful satellites were launched into space, and they continue to gather incredible information.

America joined the international space race with the launch of Explorer I in 1958.

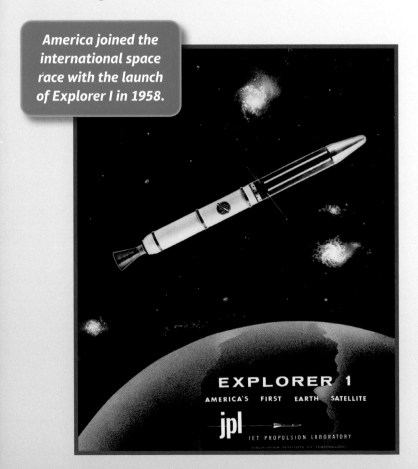

EXPLORER 1

AMERICA'S FIRST EARTH SATELLITE

jpl

JET PROPULSION LABORATORY

CALIFORNIA INSTITUTE OF TECHNOLOGY

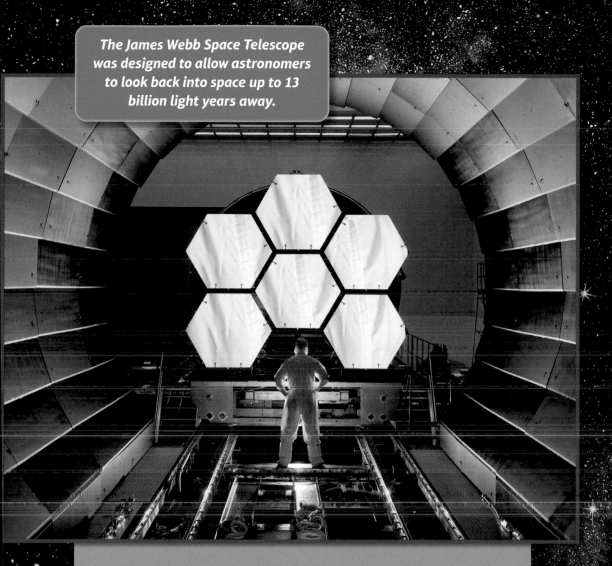

The James Webb Space Telescope was designed to allow astronomers to look back into space up to 13 billion light years away.

COSMIC TIME MACHINE

Astronomers measure vast distances in space by light years. A light year is 5.88 trillion miles (9.46 trillion km). Since objects in space are so far away, it takes a lot of time for their light to reach Earth. The farther away something is, the further in the past we see it. That's how the JWST lets scientists see back in time.

The space shuttle Discovery launched on April 24, 1990 carrying a crew of five and the Hubble Space Telescope.

FROM IDEA TO REALITY

Decades later, in 1977, Congress finally approved a plan for a large space telescope. Scientists and engineers got to work on the ambitious project. The Hubble Space Telescope was launched into space on April 24, 1990.

Since then, Hubble has revealed many space secrets. It found evidence that the universe is about 13.7 billion years old.

It discovered supersized black holes in galaxies and captured amazing images of a star being consumed in one. It helped scientists understand more about how planets are formed. It found four moons around the dwarf planet Pluto. In 2022, it captured images of a star being consumed in a black hole. Hubble is expected to continue its space investigations until 2030 or 2040.

All these discoveries made scientists want to discover more. It was time for a new idea.

The Hubble Space Telescope has made important discoveries about black holes like this possible runaway black hole creating a trail of stars.

A TALE OF TWO TELESCOPES

The James Webb Space Telescope is not meant to replace the Hubble Space Telescope. The two are teammates. They each build on the discoveries of the other.

One of Hubble's biggest jobs is to study planets in our solar system. It orbits Earth and is about the size of a large school bus. It sees the universe in ultraviolet wavelengths, a type of

The JWST is protected from the sun's rays by a five-layer sunscreen.

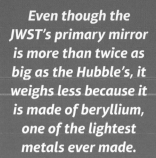

Even though the JWST's primary mirror is more than twice as big as the Hubble's, it weighs less because it is made of beryllium, one of the lightest metals ever made.

JWST primary mirror

Hubble primary mirror

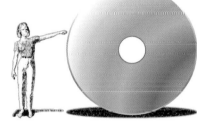

light that is not visible to human eyes. The Hubble telescope has been in orbit for well over thirty years and continues to dazzle scientists with its discoveries.

The JWST's primary mission is to study both old and new planets and stars. It orbits our sun one million miles (1.5 million km) away from Earth. It is bigger and lighter than Hubble. Its protective sunscreen is the size of half a 737 airplane. It sees the universe in infrared wavelengths, another type of light human eyes can't see.

This JWST infrared image of the Carina Nebula reveals previously invisible areas of star birth.

CHAPTER 2

A NEXT-GENERATION TELESCOPE

The Hubble telescope was such a huge success that it made scientists wonder: What if we could see even farther into space? The Hubble orbits Earth. The new idea became: Can we put a telescope into orbit around our sun?

The Hubble telescope sees in ultraviolet light. Scientists knew that a telescope that could see in infrared light could look through dust and particles that sometimes block Hubble images.

Using infrared light would provide an even more detailed look into space. In 1996, exploring this idea became an official project called Next Generation Space Telescope.

NASA put some of its most brilliant scientists and engineers to work. They took on the challenge of planning, designing, and testing all kinds of solutions. Their goal was to develop a telescope that was 100 times more powerful than Hubble.

MIRROR, MIRROR IN THE SKY

It takes a big mirror to look at galaxies more than 13 billion light years away from Earth. At 21.4 feet (21.4 m) across, the JWST's primary mirror is the largest mirror ever launched into space. All its mirrors are coated in a very thin layer of real gold to better reflect infrared light.

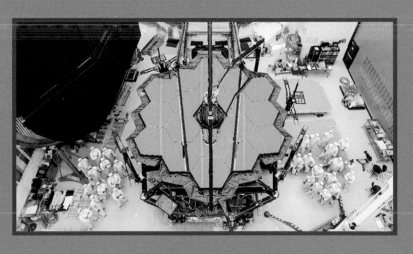

TELESCOPE TEAMWORK

The European Space Agency and Canadian Space Agency teamed up with NASA. These international partners helped with the thinking, planning, and funding. Altogether, several thousand

> *Buildilng the JWST involved people from all over the world.*

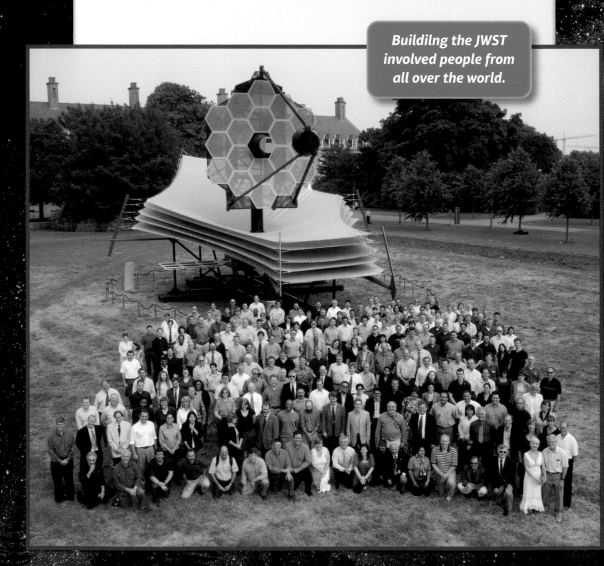

The JWST made a long journey by land and sea before it was launched into space.

scientists, engineers, and technicians from seventeen countries helped build the James Webb Space Telescope.

There was a long process of testing and mistakes and do-overs. Thirty years and $10 billion later, a ship carrying the JWST left California. It passed through the Panama Canal and arrived in French Guiana off the coast of South America on October 12, 2021.

The JWST was launched on Christmas Day in 2021 from Europe's Spaceport.

BLAST OFF!

French Guiana was chosen as an ideal launch site. It is located near the equator, where the rotation of the Earth could give the launch an extra boost. That was where the James Webb Space Telescope was successfully launched by a rocket on Christmas day in 2021. It took the JWST about a month to travel 940,000 miles (1.5 million km) to its destination near the Sun.

On July 12, 2022, NASA released the first images from the JWST and they did not disappoint. For the first time, the images revealed cosmic cliffs and sparkling young stars that gave scientists new insight into how stars are formed.

All this is just the beginning! The JWST continues to amaze the world with images from the great beyond.

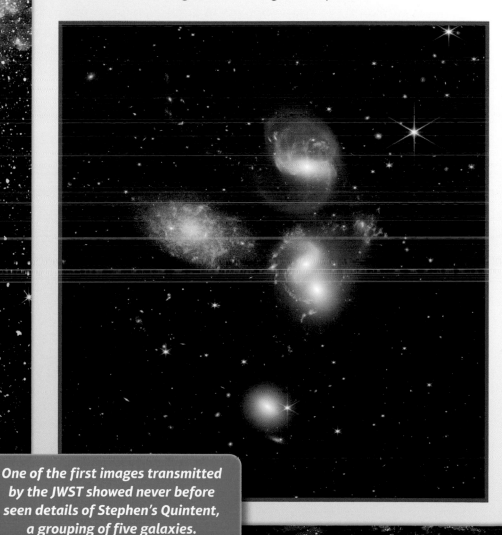

One of the first images transmitted by the JWST showed never before seen details of Stephen's Quintent, a grouping of five galaxies.

What's In a Name?

The James Webb Space Telescope is named after the man who invented it, right?

Wrong! James Webb was not even alive when his namesake telescope was built and launched.

James Webb led NASA from 1961 to 1968. When President John F. Kennedy challenged NASA to put a person on the moon by 1970, it became Webb's job to make it happen. He directed NASA's famous Apollo space program that put the first humans on the moon.

NASA administrator James Webb (right) meets with President John F. Kennedy (left) to discuss his vision for space exploration.

NASA won the space race to put the first humans on the moon.

When it came time to name the telescope, Webb's visionary leadership was remembered. Neil Armstrong was the first person who walked on the moon. He described the experience as ". . . one small step for man, one giant leap for mankind." The JWST represents another giant leap forward, made possible, in part, by Webb's earlier efforts.

The Cartwheel galaxy, captured by the JWST, got its wheel-like shape when another galaxy crashed into it.

CHAPTER 3

INTERGALACTIC DISCOVERIES

It is no wonder that the James Webb Space Telescope is considered a major science breakthrough. The telescope was all systems go in June 2022. Within days, it was delivering astounding images of both old and new galaxies that had never been seen before. Some were more than 150 million years older than those located by Hubble.

Thanks to the JWST, we have now witnessed new stars being formed and spotted some of the oldest stars in existence. The JWST lets scientists look back in time and it has confirmed the existence of the four oldest galaxies ever seen. It captured images of Jupiter and some of its moons and rings. Another exciting discovery came about when JWST tracked the movement of an asteroid for the first time.

Images released by NASA in early 2023 show a dense molecular cloud with temperatures of minus 440 degrees Fahrenheit (minus 263 degrees Celsius). These are the coldest ices ever discovered. Other images captured a pair of galaxies merging, or coming together, with each other. The collision happened about 500 million light years from Earth in the constellation Delphinus.

JWST captured two galaxies coming together.

SO MUCH TO SEE AND SHARE

The JWST captures about 68 gigabytes of new data every day. That's a bit more than an iPhone 12 can hold. Even though the telescope is located almost 1 million miles (1.6 million km) away, it takes only four and a half hours to relay information back to Earth.

All that data keeps scientists busy researching new discoveries. Every week technicians program a weekly schedule and upload it to JWST using NASA's Deep Space Network. This schedule tells the JWST when and what to observe. Competition is fierce among scientists who want to use the JWST to investigate what they are studying in space.

Engineers test the micro shutter array, a new technology used on the JWST.

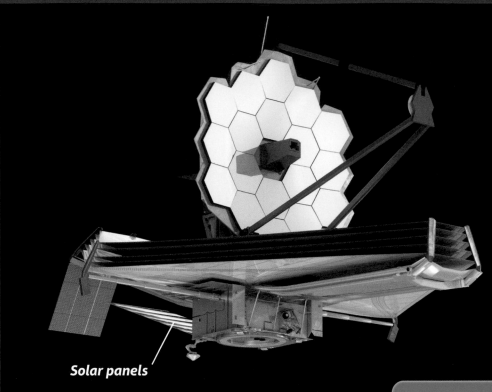

Solar panels

The JWST is powered by solar energy.

CHAPTER 4

THE GOLDEN AGE OF ASTRONOMY

Scientists are awed by what the JWST has already revealed and are eager to learn more. What will it tell us about the building blocks of life? What can we learn about dust storms, weather patterns, and seasons on Mars? How are exoplanets (planets

SOLAR POWER

JWST orbits around the Sun. With so much energy nearby, it is no surprise that it is powered by solar energy. Solar panels supply power to all its scientific instruments, communications, and propulsion systems. What is a surprise? The JWST needs only one kilowatt of energy to keep it running smoothly. That's about how much power it takes to microwave your lunch!

that orbit other stars) like Earth? Every discovery brings new understanding and raises new questions.

NASA has its sights set on Mars.

Night rendering of what the Giant Magellan Telescope is expected to look like.

ONLY THE BEGINNING

The James Webb Space Telescope continues to prove that the universe is bigger and more exciting than we ever imagined. Now the big question is: What comes next?

As is often the case, one good idea gives way to another. As incredible as the JWST is proving to be, plans are underway for even bigger and stronger telescopes. Be on the lookout for the Giant Magellan Telescope. It is expected to be ready in 2029. Its designers say it will be 200 times more powerful than existing research telescopes.

What will astronomers find in the skies next?

GLOSSARY

asteroid: a small, rocky object that orbits the Sun

astrophysicist: a scientist who studies space, stars, planets, and the universe

black hole: an area of space where a collapsed star is squeezed in so tightly and gravity is so strong that nothing, including light, can escape

infrared: light that falls just outside the visual spectrum, beyond the range of what humans see as red

meteor: a piece of rock or metal from outer space that speeds into Earth's atmosphere and looks like a streak of light

National Aeronautics and Space Agency (NASA): a United States government agency that specializes in space exploration

satellite: a spacecraft launched into orbit around the Earth, Sun, a moon, or another planet to collect information or monitor communication

telescope: an instrument that makes distant objects seem larger and closer; it can be used to study space

ultraviolet: a type of light that cannot be seen by the human eye, beyond the range of what humans see as violet

LEARN MORE

Britannica Kids: James Webb Space Telescope
https://kids.britannica.com/students/article/James-Webb-Space-Telescope/634461

Kiddle: James Webb Space Telescope Facts for Kids
https://kids.kiddle.co/James_Webb_Space_Telescope

The Kids Should See This: This Is a Film About the James Webb Space Telescope
https://thekidshouldseethis.com/post/james-webb-space-telescope-hainline-smilemountain-film

Mann, Dionna L. *Hidden Heroes in Space Exploration*. Minneapolis: Lerner Publications, 2023.

NASA: What is the James Webb Telescope?
https://spaceplace.nasa.gov/james-webb-space-telescope/en

Schaefer, Lola M. *Explore Telescopes*. Minneapolis: Lerner Publications, 2023.

Stratton, Connor. *Space Exploration*. Lake Elmo, MN: Focus Readers, 2023.

Tyson, Neil deGrasse, with Gregory Mone. *Astrophysics for Young People in a Hurry*. New York: Norton Young Readers, 2019.

INDEX

PHOTO ACKNOWLEDGMENTS

p. 4-5; Tithi Luadthong/Shutterstock, p.6; Dima Zel/Shutterstock, p.7; fcdb/iStock, p. 8; NASA/JPL, p. 9; NASA/David Higginbotham, p. 10; NASA, p. 11; NASA/ESA/ Leah Hustak (STScI), p. 12; NASA/Chris Gunn, p. 13; NASA, p. 14; NASA/ESA/CSA/ STScI, p. 15; NASA/Johnson Space Center, p. 16; NASA, p. 17; NASA/Chris Gunn, p.18; NASA/Chris Gunn, p. 19; NASA/ESA/CSA/STScI, p.20; Abbie Rowe/White House Photographs/John F. Kennedy Presidential Library and Museum, p. 21; Castleski/ Shutterstock, p. 22; NASA/ESA/CSA/STScI, p. 23; NASA/ESA, p. 24; NASA/Chris Gunn, p. 25; NASA Goddard/Chris Gunn, p. 26; NASA/Northrup Grommon, p. 27; Vadim Sadovski, p. 28; Giant Magellan Telescope/GMTO Corporation, p. 29; AstroStar/ Shutterstock.

Cover (background): alex-mit/iStock
Cover (image): Maria Starovoytova/Shutterstock
Interior (background): Sergey Nivens/Shutterstock